Jobs People Do

Librarians

by Emily Raij

PEBBLE
a capstone imprint

Pebble Explore is published by Pebble, an imprint of Capstone.
1710 Roe Crest Drive
North Mankato, Minnesota 56003
www.capstonepub.com

Library of Congress Cataloging-in-Publication Data is available on the Library of Congress website.
ISBN: 978-1-9771-1376-4 (library binding)
ISBN: 978-1-9771-1811-0 (paperback)
ISBN: 978-1-9771-1384-9 (eBook PDF)

Summary: Librarians keep books and other materials at libraries organized and help people find what they need. Learn all the roles librarians have, the tools they use, and how people get this job.

Image Credits
Alamy: AztecBlue, 10, 19 (middle), Ian Lamond, 8, JeffG, 9, Randy Duchaine, 7; Capstone Studio: Karon Dubke, 11; Dreamstime: Gan Hui, 1; iStockphoto: FangXiaNuo, 5, FatCamera, 23, 27, kali9, 21, miodrag ignjatovic, 17, Steve Debenport, 12, 13, 25; Newscom: Reuters/Atef Hassan, 28, ZUMA Press/Joan Barnett Lee, 15, ZUMA Press/Lannis Waters, 19 (bottom), ZUMA Press/San Diego Union-Tribune, 18; Shutterstock: Dariusz Jarzabek, 19 (top left), Fotosoroka, 19 (top right), Rawpixel.com, 6, 22, Tyler Olson, Cover, 14, wavebreakmedia, 24

Editorial Credits
Editor: Carrie Sheely; Designer: Kyle Grenz; Media Researcher: Jo Miller; Production Specialist: Kathy McColley

Consultant Credits
Katy Hiltner, Head Librarian
Hutchinson and Winsted Public Libraries
Pioneerland Library System

Printed and bound in the USA.
PA99

Table of Contents

Words in **bold** are in the glossary.

What Is a Librarian?

You walk into a library. You want a book to read. Where can you find it? You ask the librarian. She helps you find it. She helps you check out the book. Then you can bring it home.

Librarians work in libraries. They help you find books. They help you use library computers to find information too. They help you find whatever you need!

The United States has more than 100,000 libraries. Libraries have a lot of books. But that's not all they have. Libraries have other resources. These include newspapers and magazines. Some libraries have movies and music **recordings**.

Many libraries have **e-books**. E-books are electronic books. You can read them on the screen of a computer or another **device**.

Librarians keep track of everything at a library. They help people find and use the resources.

Where Librarians Work

Librarians work in different kinds of libraries. Your school probably has a library. Librarians there help students. They may see hundreds of students a day!

Have you been to a library in your town? This is a public library. Anyone can use this library.

a public library

A museum librarian shows some history books.

Librarians work for **colleges**, museums, and other places too. Museums often keep art or important things from long ago. Some librarians work at **hospital** libraries. Librarians there often study, or research. They tell other hospital workers what they learned.

What Librarians Do

How do librarians keep all the books in order? They use call numbers. Each book has a call number on its **spine**. People use call numbers to find books.

spine

call number

A librarian sets up a display of craft books.

Sometimes librarians set out books for displays. They might set out books at special times of the year. People who see these books may want to read them.

Librarians help others find books
that interest them. If you like sharks,
the librarian might tell you about a
shark book.

Librarians help people check out books and other **materials**. Then the items can be taken home. People need a library card to check out materials. A librarian can help people get their library cards.

To check out materials, a librarian uses a **scanner**. Each library card has its own number. It shows who owns the card. The librarian scans the library card and what is being checked out. At some libraries, people can check out their own items. After being checked out, the materials are ready to take home.

A librarian uses a scanner to check out books.

Some libraries have places where visitors can check out books themselves.

People must return materials to the library. The librarian scans the returned items. Then the librarian puts the materials back on shelves. Then they can be checked out again.

Librarians choose materials for the library. They read book reviews that people wrote. The reviews help them find out about new books. A review tells them if people who have read a book liked it. Librarians also learn about their visitors. They choose books people want to check out.

Librarians buy materials. They only have a certain amount of money to spend. They make choices about how to spend it.

When new books come in, librarians enter each book in the **catalog**. The catalog is a list of materials a library has. It is kept on a computer. Librarians put a call number and other labels on each book. They put the books on carts. Then they put the books on the shelves.

A librarian puts on book labels.

Tools Librarians Use

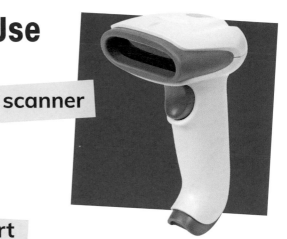

scanner

book cart

book labels

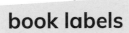

Librarians also plan events for the library. Some have movie nights. Others hold book clubs. People in these groups meet to talk about books they read.

Librarians might have a book writer, or author, come to the library. The author talks about his or her book.

Librarians also might have story times. They read books to kids at story times.

Some librarians teach classes. They might teach computer classes. These classes help people learn how to use computers. School librarians might teach classes on how to use the library's resources.

A librarian teaches a class.

School and public librarians might set up makerspaces. These are areas for people to make things. They have art supplies and tools to use.

Librarians keep track of all library materials. They keep track of how much people are using certain books. This helps them know what to buy. They take old and damaged books off shelves. They might take off books that people don't check out a lot too.

Librarians also keep computers
and other equipment ready to use.
They learn how it works so they can
help users.

How to Become a Librarian

It takes a lot of training to become a librarian. Most people go to a college for four years to get a **degree**.

Many people then go on to get another degree. This usually takes two or more years. Students take classes that teach them to work at a library.

School librarians often have to take a state test. They then get a license to work in a school.

Famous Librarians

Some librarians became well known. Laura Bush was a librarian. She is the wife of past U.S. president George W. Bush. She helped set up the National Book Festival.

Alia Muhammad Baker was a librarian in Iraq. She worried about her library being wrecked in a war in 2003. She saved about 30,000 books before the library was destroyed.

Alia Muhammad Baker

Fast Facts

- **What Librarians Do:**
  Librarians help people get information and materials. They keep library materials organized.

- **Where Librarians Work:**
  school libraries, public libraries, college libraries, other libraries

- **Key Tools:**
  scanners, computers, book carts, book labels

- **Education Needed:**
  four years of college; many people go to school for about two more years for another degree; school librarians often need a license

- **Famous Librarians:**
  Laura Bush, Alia Muhammad Baker

Glossary

catalog (CAT-uh-log)—the list of all the materials in a library stored on a computer

college (KOL-ij)—a school that students go to after high school

degree (di-GREE)—proof of graduating from college

device (de-VISSE)—equipment that does a certain job

e-book (EE-buk)—a book that is stored so it can be read on a computer or other device

hospital (HOSS-pi-tuhl)—a place where doctors and others work to help people who are sick or hurt

material (muh-TIHR-ee-uhl)—an item that people can look at in libraries or check out of libraries

recording (ri-KOR-ding)—sounds, music, or other content stored to use later

scanner (SKAN-ur)—a machine that moves a beam of light over a number and sends the information to a computer

spine (SPINE)—the part of a book to which the pages are attached

Read More

Austen, Mary. *Librarians on the Job.* New York: KidHaven Press, 2017.

Hoena, Blake A. *The Library: A 4-D Book.* North Mankato, MN: Capstone Press, 2018.

Kenan, Tessa. *Hooray for Librarians!* Minneapolis: Lerner Publishing, 2018.

Internet Sites

American Library Association: Careers in Librarianship: For Kids
http://www.ala.org/educationcareers/careers/librarycareerssite/kids

Library of Congress: Kids
http://read.gov/kids/

Index